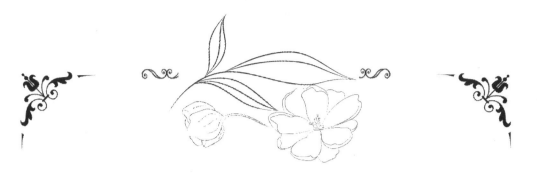

This Book Belongs To :

D1567680

Welcome

TO

Your 90 days of Positive Affirmations

Workbook

Instructions:

Read the positive affirmation at the top of each page.
Write the thoughts that come to your mind when you
read the prompt. Fill the space or write a sentence or two.
There are no wrong answers, and you can complete the
pages in any order.

There are 90 days of prompts provided and pages for
notes in the back of the book. Also included is a page for
your final thoughts.

Good things are coming my way.

I take pleasure in my own solitude.

I execute my plan and produce expected results.

I am the architect of my life.

I build its foundation and choose its contents.

I am blessed with incredible friends.

Everything in my life has a purpose.

I will work on seeing only the positives and block
out the negatives of life.

I help others see their worth.

I may not understand the good in this situation,
but it is there.

I am worthy of love.

I can do anything that I set my mind too.

I am my best source of motivation.

I love who I am.

I am proud to be me.

I enjoy my own company.

The past has no power over me anymore.

I cannot give up until I have tried every conceivable way.

I deserve admiration.

There is a good reason I was paired
with this perfect family.

There is a great reason this is unfolding
before me now.

I am a money magnet
and attract wealth and abundance.

This situation works out for my highest good.

I am doing work that I enjoy and find fulfilling.

I am a better person from the hardship
that I've gone through with my family.

I have the smarts and the ability
to get through this.

I am worth loving.

I am a unique child of this world.

I am a good person at all times of day and night.

I choose to see the light that I am to this world.

This day will be a gorgeous day to remember.

I compare myself only to my highest self.

I play the biggest role in my own career success.

I can kindly ask for help and guidance
if I cannot see a better way.

This situation works out for my highest good.

I offer an apology to those affected by my anger.

I show compassion in helping my loved ones understand my dreams.

I muster up more hope and courage
from deep inside me.

I dance to the music that is my own life.

I am doing work that I enjoy and find fulfilling.

I may not understand the good in this situation,
but it is there.

I must know what awaits me at the end of this path, so I do not give up.

I take the time to show my friends
that I care about them.

I let go of my anger so I can see clearly.

I refuse to give up because I haven't tried all possible ways.

The answer is right before me,
even if I am not seeing it yet.

I follow my dreams no matter what.

I am safe and sound. All is well.

I make the right choices every time.

I am deeply fulfilled with who I am.

This day brings me nothing but joy.

I matter and what I have to offer this world also matters.

I see myself as a gift to my people
and community and world.

I let go of worries that drain my energy.

I draw from my inner strength and light.

I adopt the mindset of praising myself.

I answer questions about my dreams
without getting defensive.

I engage in work that impacts
this world positively.

I have as much brightness to offer the world
as the next person.

I surround myself with people
who treat me well.

I take great pleasure in my friends,
even if they disagree or live different lives.

I embrace diversity in my life.

I replace my anger with understanding
and compassion.

I know my wisdom guides me
to the right decision.

All my problems have a solution.

Giving up is easy and always an option,
so let's delay it for another day.

I accept everyone as they are and continue on with pursuing my dream.

I focus on breathing and grounding myself.

I breathe in calmness
and breathe out nervousness.

I trust my inner wisdom and intuition.

I am more than good enough,
and I get better every day.

I love and approve of myself.

I listen lovingly to this inner conflict and reflect on it until I get to peace around it.

I am happy in my own skin
and in my own circumstances.

All that I need comes to me at the right time
and place in this life.

I release my mind of thought until the morning.

I trust myself to make the best decision for me.

The past has no power over me anymore. I embrace the rhythm and the flowing of my own heart.

I forgive myself for all the mistakes I have made.

I let go of worries that drain my energy.

I have no right to compare myself to anyone
for I do not know their whole story.

I show my family how much I love them
in all the verbal and non-verbal ways I can.

I cannot give up until I have tried every conceivable way.

I choose friends who approve of me
and love me.

I receive all feedback with kindness
but make the final call myself.

My thoughts are my reality,
so I think up a bright new day.

I seek a new way of thinking about this situation.

I fill my day with hope and face it with joy.

I ask my loved ones to support my dreams.

Everything works out for my highest good.

I fully approve of who I am,
even as I get better.

My Notes

My Notes

My Notes

My Notes

My Notes

My Notes

My Final Thoughts

Made in the USA
Middletown, DE
18 December 2022

19511053R00062